CRUSHING CORRUPTION:
Draining The California Swamp

ERIN CRUZ

Copyright © 2019 by Erin Cruz

All rights reserved. No part of this publication may be reproduced, distributed, or transmitted in any form or by any means, including photocopying, recording, or other electronic or mechanical methods, without the prior written permission of the publisher, except in the case of brief quotations embodied in critical reviews and certain other noncommercial uses permitted by copyright law.

For permission requests, write to the publisher, addressed "Attention: Permissions Coordinator," at the address below.

Erin Cruz, Inc.
8690 Aero Drive
Ste 115-304
San Diego, CA 92123

www.erincruz.com

Printed in the United States of America

ISBN: 9781799280651

DEDICATION

This evolving book is dedicated to all of the beautiful and wonderful people who have helped crush corruption in California and across the nation. Never give up. Never. This book is for you. We are just beginning.

CONTENTS

	Prologue	i
Chapter 1:	Bot Boss Mamma	1
Chapter 2:	Swamp Monsters	12
Chapter 3:	Collision of Collusion & Commie Crawlers	59
Chapter 4:	Swamp Busters	67

To be continued ….

PROLOGUE

There is nothing like a Presidential Election gone right. At times we don't know what we need until the fog clears and we can see what is right in front of our noses and out on the horizon, blinking our eyes to adjust our focus. In 2016, the Presidential Election cycle sent the nation into a frenzy. There is no difference if you are Republican or Democrat the aforementioned statement is true. Think about that statement for a moment. Perhaps your blood is boiling already thinking about where this story is going. Blue wave or Red wave, ride it and follow along.

Let's rewind. Rewind to the point in time when the candidate selection was narrowed. In the beginning of 2016, the pool was looking to be Hillary Clinton vs John Kasich, Marco Rubio, Ted Cruz, or Donald J. Trump -- maybe. Now, here is the deal – if we knew then what we know now… I will let you finish that statement. In all seriousness, we don't have hindsight, so we go with what we have at that point. 2016 brought a whirlwind of scandals, accusations, mud throwing, all out fights on social media, insult slapping, you name it, it pretty much happened. It wasn't pretty, not from either side of the isle. Again, no matter what side you are on, this is likely seen as truth.

So where is this all going? I have been deeply involved in politics now for a decade, and at that time, the time of reducing the candidate pool down within the Republican Party, I witnessed something that I never could have conceived possible. We will come back to *that* "Swamp Buster" moment a bit later. Now, in the knock out, drag down verbal shootouts, Donald J. Trump mentioned the "Swamp" and Ted Cruz described something similar, referring to it as "The Washington Cartel." Name it what you like, dress it up and make it fancy, but at that time, unless you were in the "inner circles" throughout the states and regions and within the national political spectrum you likely didn't see it, but for a glimpse portrayed by two dueling tongue slingers. O.K., six of them. I did, and clearly. Even if for a mere five minutes, it wasn't pretty. I am not one to let corruption roll on. Later on, in the story I will get into it deeper.

This is where my gut, my inner being, the core of who I am, couldn't just stand by and watch any longer. Now was the time for me to get even deeper involved locally and online. More and more, as the candidates dwindled, my vision and clarity for what was really happening within our Republic, within my own political party, locally and nationally, became my own reality. The reality of my children, the reality of my future grandchildren was literally at stake. Enough was enough.

My activism has always been local, but "big picture" is my talent. Given the "big picture" gift, national politics is my forte. There was a great deal going on locally, but our nation needed strong fighters and influencers helping Donald J. Trump spread his message in order to win against the "Clinton Machine." So, there I was at the edge of the political "swamp" and facing the "Washington Cartel," California style, do I go for it? Absolutely. Both feet. Jump in and GO! Praise the Lord many thousands of other patriots were also willing to answer the call. Rise up! And we did.

Swinging in full force, mud flying everywhere, especially from the "Clinton Machine." For me, that was a bit of a shocker. I am not a fan of Hillary Clinton. No, I am not. Hillary Clinton is a notable First Lady who is well respected by many. She is also feared by those who view her as monster surrounded by death scandals. And then there are her husband's sexual scandals, her brazen need to defend him and protect him. Top it all off with her lengthy history, one would gather she would run a clean and classy race, right? Wrong.

The range was drastic, from sexual accusations of Donald J. Trump to more dirt and mudslinging about clothing, styles of attire and hairstyles, on both sides, from both candidates. It was WILD! Almost as wild as The Donald's hair and Hill-Bill's whacky pant suits? Almost. You see? Now, I can't help but laugh at the horrifying pettiness in the Presidential Election. We must learn and grow from this last election. We must! Even I can admit I love a great flash pantsuit and big hair.

Why does everything have to be divisive?

It doesn't, unless you are in politics for financial and power gain, or you are in the media and want a meal ticket.

Just disgusting.

The only way to solve the problem is to be a part of the solution. We will get back to that later.

Yes, Donald J. Trump won the Primary Election in 2016. Finally. Life in politics had never been so dramatic, energizing, and fun, from the Republican Perspective. Unless you are a "Never Trumper" Republican, but just like a big dysfunctional family, something has got to give, and I really wanted to play a part helping the solution.

The time was right to really engage utilizing my communication tools developed for activists, put them to the real test. Not only was I active on the National Level with the Presidential Election, I was active state-wide helping with various races behind the scenes, networking, learning about the ins and outs of "The California Swamp."

It was quite the eye-opener. Many are in "it," in politics, but somehow, they can't see "IT." This for me was a strange phenomenon. Or, perhaps they conveniently don't see "it." Either way, something was really off. There was one race in particular, where I was able to see through the "lens" clearly and figure out that our entire system here in California and perhaps even the entire Republic is corrupted. When I moved forward to run for United States Senate in late 2017 it became crystal clear our Republic is Strong, unfortunately it is corrupted by the corrupt. The same goes for the Republican Party. The party platform is solid, the people in the party, many are what I now call swamp monsters they need a "Come to Jesus" moment and to be brought back from the dead or they need to move on from a platform which doesn't align with their corrupt ways.

Swamp busters were brought together in January 2018 to help the fight to restore California and our great Republic.

This is where our story really begins. Some of the story may not be palatable to you; perhaps you might find the information bothersome or disturbing. Trust me, this is not the intent. You might laugh through the book or roll your eyes. It might be funny, it may be frightening, and much of the book is figurative or representative. The truth is this, what I aim to share with you is information which will help you understand what is really going on within the belly of the beast of politics and expose the Monsters within who are a true and real threat to not only our parties, but to the Republic of California and the United States of America as a whole.

If I could be one to run up and down the state, declaring, "The communists are coming, the communists are coming!" and save the State of California, I would. In fact, I have, and then some. People need to wake up. The issue is, the communists are already here! Please, read the last sentence again. Yes, they are here and my aim, and the aim of the Swamp busters is to expose them all.

This is a courageous act I am told, to share my story. To me this is not my story it is our story. I must share with you what I have learned. Know though, I have to side with caution so the characters within my book are representative and not named in entirety, nor are they distinctly identified in every case. So, is this a true story? Is it? You will have to decide. You will have to determine if you will become a Swamp Buster or become a Swamp Monster. Trust you, me, this story will not be over even by the time you read it, perhaps even ten years from now, or even twenty.

Our Republic is in the fight of its life to retain Liberty, to keep the Freedom bell Ringing.

CHAPTER ONE
BOT BOSS MAMMA

Once upon a time there was a President and his name was Barack Hussein Obama. We throw back to the time of online keyboard warriors in pop up chat rooms, twitter, social media pages, and forums throughout the country taking to their new found first amendment speech going viral in an instant with the clickity clack of keyboards and mice everywhere. The pound sign on the keyboard soon became a modality of trend filtering and received a new name: hash tag. Now, many call it a "hash."

It was then, under Barack Obama we heard a President speak out against his constituents. Obama verbally and politically went against those who opposed his policies, calling them names. In my life I couldn't recall such an instance happening. For me, it was deeply disrespectful toward over half of the population who didn't support his radical policies. Nonetheless, he did it. He insulted and went into the gutter and stayed there for eight long years.

Some might say it wasn't that bad when the prodding, name

calling, and jabbing started from the Presidential Pulpit, but the reality of a sitting President insulting and striking out at those who oppose him, not the political elite, but the actual people, it was the start of Chicago style political rule. Witnessing the outright harsh and corrupted tactics of thug style organizations being used and in our highest office was an eye-opener for many.

The most difficult situation of a leader and political activist was watching regular everyday people get so frustrated because not only were socialist policies shoved through against the peoples will, these same people were forced to pay his salary, month after month, and year after year. It was beyond disturbing, it also drove Americans to work harder to communicate the message of freedom.

You are asking, I know, what did he do? What was it he said? Barack Obama came out and called Republicans online and throughout the nation, "The Mob." Immediately patriots across the country fired back, declaring a new hash tag #WeAreTheMOB. The fury was not to be stopped and with the many hot ticket progressive policies Obama was putting forth, "the mob" was fed up and on fire for freedom and protecting and defending their free speech. Not Chicago style thug politics, not "Alinsky Tactics" would stop what was to come and what is currently on fire throughout the land currently.

We The People were fired up. About this time the rallies in Washington D.C. and nationwide pop up rallies were happening. The country was ignited for the fight of their lives. We saw groups from left leaning organizations and even Independent affiliated groups joining in protests with the right, including moderates, and Republicans. People from all walks, who love freedom started sharing information on what was really going on behind the Obama communist curtain. Pretty much, Obama had pinned himself and other Progressives against a wall. Even with the AP and Obama's team filtering all Administration Output in terms of what the public was offered, and force fed, the people were still able to get enough data out to expose those behind the Obama Administration Agenda.

It wasn't long after Obama came out and started pushing back against those who were sharing the information he didn't want shared, I recall someone on the social media platform, Twitter, calling me the "Mob Boss." And then it turned into the "Mob Boss Mamma!" At the time I didn't think much of it, but it was there and a huge compliment looking back. To be considered one who many look to for information, share private information with, to be a facilitator, and one who would stand alongside the U. S. Constitution, and on the side of Liberty and Freedom when it certainly wasn't a safe space to do so outwardly – it was my honor.

The reality then, and even the reality now, we were not "the mob" or a thug group or organization or anything close to what one might think the "mob" would actually consist of. Obama was doing what his ilk have done now for over a decade. The exact tactic and Swamp Weapon used, we will discuss that later. To give you a glimpse now, the Swamp Monsters insult, point fingers, shout, "You are the Mob!"

Why? Because they are the "mob" and they do not want anyone to look at what they are doing which is likely the same exact variation which they accuse others of doing!

If you step back a moment, look objectively at what we have witnessed in recent history. Look at the interactions from all angles. We have seen this tactical maneuver used over and over and over again since the Obama Administration Era, though it existed long, long before. There are various versions of this tactic displayed in recent history and degrees it is used varies. Many factors play into the entire Swamp Monster and Swamp Arsenal. This is another reason I will share with you what I have learned first-hand, another reason for writing this book. History repeats. If we can evolve, anticipate, stay vigilant, we can combat human corruption effectively.

These evil and manipulative types will continue to exist, their tactics and weapons will continue to be used. Something which this "Bot Boss Mamma" has been looking at and researching over the last year is the relevance of those using the Swamp Monster tactics to deflect, project, interject, provide misinformation, disinformation, and disturb the normal and functional flow of humanity and order in the United States. It seems even those on the "right" side of good and evil just don't seem to get "it" or do they and are they actually part of the Swamp? The reason I mention this is somehow those on the right, conservatives, republicans, even the independents are slow to even acknowledge tactics are used, deep imbedded corruption exists let alone is an issue, that these tactics are being used by the

Swamp Monsters on the left. This is something which must change, and now.

For a decade I have worn the "#IamTheMob" and "#MobBossMamma" badge of honor. I can only hope to help lead We The People to truth and assist in retaining our God given Liberties and Freedoms from the grips of Government, the elitist multinational corporation thugs who wish to regulate every area of our lives.

Interestingly enough, it wasn't until I ran for U.S. Senate against Dianne Feinstein when the "mob" and "boss mamma" came full circle! This story I will also elaborate on later. For now, the short version is enough to help you gather thoughts on how imbedded our political operatives are, how corrupted our system has become, and the Swamp Monsters, just how scary, evil, and outright crazy they are.

There is a need to have all of the Swamp Monsters in government and within party leadership positions removed from office or positions of power as soon as possible, be it indictments carried out or the ballot box put to full use by all those folks who cherish their liberty and freedom, even committees shifting their priorities, it needs to happen.

While what you are reading seems odd and topical, the truths spoken are just that. Not only truth, they are built on the understanding my run for U.S. Senate would be against someone who is considered one of the most corrupt career politicians of all time. This someone who started her massive life-long political career being ushered into office as Mayor when another politician was removed from office via assassination[1]. Chilling way to get a job.

We don't believe in coincidences, especially when they repeat. Recently San Francisco saw a vacancy of their Mayor, again. Not that San Francisco has seen an assassination of their most recent Mayor in 2018, rather he died of a heart incident.

The next Mayor? Appointed.

That seems to be how the Corrupt Bay Area Swamp works. Who is she? A staunch progressive liberal woman of color. Checking the diversity boxes. Can you say, agenda approved? Picture perfect Swamp Monster? This is such a tragedy for San Francisco especially given the community is facing the highest levels of homelessness, crime, housing prices are through the roof and there is a mass exodus from the region. San Franciscans never seem to have a clean election where the people get to have their elected heard in the public square and consequently the people's will expressed at the ballot box. Clean. Instead the cycle continues.

Back to the "Bot Boss Mamma" story. It was about half way through our campaign for U.S. Senate when the crazy kooky left started screaming from the rooftop there are "BOTS" on twitter, the "BOTS" are from Russia and they are undermining our elections. In fact, this was being yelled long after Donald J. Trump became our President. Some of the talk was pointing to pre-election of Donald J.

Trump and insinuating that this "BOT" activity caused a tear-jerking loss of the Presidency for Hillary Clinton.

Call the wambulance, no – not a chance. But when you looked closer and followed the vibration of the "BOT" chatter from the highest level of the Creepy Crawler Swamp Monsters, the "bots" on Twitter cries were coming from our very own Senator Dianne Feinstein. Just then, the ringing of the ears started for my team of volunteers who reached nationwide. Yes, Feinstein was first complaining and screaming about how "Bots" were helping Trump and then moved to point out there were still bots on Twitter.

Feinstein erased her tweet where she called out that there were many "bots" in California affecting her election and interfering in the free process and sharing of information. Really?! "Bots?"

Folks, those California Activists helping in the California Elections were not "Bots" they were Volunteers! Many of them were my volunteers, people I have personally met, live-in-the-flesh, real and live human …BOTS! An army of them!

At this point we were approaching 30 million impressions weekly with our top team and no advertising on Social Media, mostly Twitter. It may be that Feinstein couldn't conceive a small-town, regular woman and mother, not a rich elitist could rally Californians and the nation to help fight for California and bring fire to the State in a positive reach for a turnover of career politicians—with little to no funding. This is when I believe she shifted tactics in the underground Swampiest of Sewers. Back to the passive attack.

YES! She was essentially calling our team of volunteers "BOTS!" Well, she wasn't alone. It seems there was a huge uptick in software and algorithms as well as apps, which were quickly developed.

Seriously, this was disturbing.

This is still disturbing. As of this writing the number of applications engaging in targeted accounts of election volunteers online is only growing.

Where did the funding come from for this massive uptick to attack our campaign? Was media investigating this? Not that we know of. Was congress looking at this or watching this? Not that we are aware of. We may never know, though we spoke about it openly in speeches, online, nearly anywhere we could where people would take this issue seriously. Only many folks didn't take this seriously and it is a huge issue, one where it definitely impacted my campaign for Federal office and my run for United States Senate. I view this as a dry run for use in a Presidential Election. Why slow free speech when you can outright silence it.

What we discovered was a vivid methodology well thought out from several angles to combat regular people on twitter expressing their minds and those who are working on political campaigns. The goal isn't to necessarily silence the person speaking, unless enough people report and block them, something which may have been able to be accomplished using some applications.

The Discovery: There are actual smart phone applications out there in Google[2] naming my volunteer team members and myself as "Bots" and displaying "Bot" type activity. No joke. This is serious from our perspective as a campaign. There have been articles on the applications as well.[3]

It was an honor to think we were so efficient and streamlined we were mimicking computers, automated programs? WOW! Way to go Team!

Yes, I made a public statement we were honored to be so efficient but mortified there would be perversion of information to the point of leading folks to think actual people were not real and their actions or motivations and intent were anything but honorable. These individuals or corporations running the "Bot" filters and blocker applications should be, in my view, investigated, as they appear to target certain groups, mainly election related.

Was Dianne Feinstein tied to or involved in the influencing of such schemes, we may never know. The timing was highly suspect. We do want to make mention people of Feinstein's high caliber and level of influence can drive markets, schemes, and people by making a simple statement publicly. Power and influence shouldn't be used maliciously for personal or political gain. To that end, shame on Senator Dianne Feinstein for leading the conversation against actual people who were volunteering, especially those who are constituents as residents of California.

As a campaign we were shut down, slowed, stalled, targeted from multiple angles. The resistance came from somewhere, it didn't just appear from nowhere, much like the hell we went through under Obama when We the People started to push back. With all of the BOT busting, our exposing the media bias and the political posturing by Feinstein and other politicos, taking on head to head battles with big media hits on our teams being "Bots," applications targeting our teams with mass block software, even Twitter shutting me and my team down for "Bot" like behaviors, and also combating the suppression and suspensions of our accounts, many recalled little ole me of old, the "#MobBossMamma" and they changed my nick name to "#BotBossMamma!"

Thank you, it is an honor. Fight on, patriots! Fight on!

Though Feinstein never mentioned me or my campaign by name, or the names of the members the Erin Cruz for U.S. Senate Team, it became increasingly clear from the outset of our campaign those on Feinstein's Team were watching and would do anything and everything to prevent clarity of information, and the advancement of our campaign. Anything. There are no limits. In fact, we have come to the conclusion they helped us to advance the non-advancement. That is the Swamp. Murky, mushy, dirty, slimy, sticky, smelly, and putrid in every way. Not a believer? Just wait. We are just getting started.

Keep in mind, some of the most real and disturbing things in life are either so simple they are overlooked and unbelievable by nature of disbelief or they are so complex there is no conceivable way that one could conceivably conceive something so complex and disgusting could be thought up by mere man.

When you get to the point where the latter is happening and you begin to think man couldn't possibly come up with such schemes and disgusting plots, just remember the reviews of the newest rendition of the movie, "It.[4]"

Some men are corrupted, others are corrupt, and there are those willing to risk everything to expose them. A brave act indeed! Something this Bot Boss Mamma will continue to do unapologetically.

CHAPTER TWO
SWAMP MONSTERS

Bravery and courage, these are both words I have heard over the course of the last year. The date of this writing is November of 2018.

Just one year ago I was minding my own business, going about the everyday life and world of an impassioned political activist. After swinging out of the hot button race of the Make America Great Again election of now President Donald J. Trump, it was clear California was one of the few states with top leadership pushing back against the America First platform and initiatives, which were extremely fruitful for many other states.

One plus one does not equal ten. It was in that moment when I was talking with a longtime friend about the direction California was moving. This dear friend asked me, "Erin, who are you and I going to vote for against Diane Feinstein?"

This gave me moment for pause.

I didn't know.

Like many people do, I had to research the candidates and we talked about this. Now, this remarkable woman responded to me with another question. She asked me if I had considered running for United States Senate.

Me? Yes, me.

So, I did my research, I looked, and I couldn't find anyone I could vote for who was running for office in the U.S. Senate race.

At that time there were over 29 people in the race. Twenty-nine.

The Swamp Monsters were busting at the seams in the candidate pool for this race! As a matter of fact, many people may recall the hot bill SB54, the California Bill put forth which was intended to protect criminal Illegal Aliens. The bill, SB54 would prevent law enforcement from notifying Federal Agents when Illegal Aliens are arrested.

In addition, after the Illegal Alien has served their time, when it came to release them, the prison, the police and officials no longer would have to notify Federal Agents and authorities when the Illegal Alien was to be taken out of containment and released into the public within the State of California.

SB54 became law and was put forth; its author was one of the candidates who were in the race for United States Senate. For those not familiar, the author of SB54 is Kevin Leon, a former State

Senator in the state of California. He most recently calls himself Kevin de Leon when his name is Kevin Alexander Leon[5].

He changed his name.

Many say this is to make him more relatable to the Hispanic groups within the state. For us, we call Kevin Leon, or as we will call him, "KL," something far different. KL is what we call a Commie Crawler in our Teams. It is beyond conceivable a man could put forth legislation that is in direct conflict with the United States Constitution and a "law" that puts all law-abiding United States Citizens at risk.

What relation does this person who is pro-Illegal Alien and pro-open borders have with communism? KL holds many positions relating to policy where the objective of the legislation and new "laws" is to bleed the California coffers dry. Literally. Call his objectives humanitarian, helping the needy, aiding those under-represented groups, others won't, but the reality is far more fierce.

KL policies put those who are not legally supposed to be in the United States as a funding priority before those persons who are United States Citizens including our homeless, mentally ill, our veterans and our own citizen children whose families have come across hard times. Further, his Commie Crawler derelict ways go further left than helping Illegal Aliens, he would like to see Medicare for All[6] bleed California and Californians dry[7].

This to me, is unacceptable. Socialism and Communism have never worked. Not to mention the principles and value systems our great Republic was built on and from.

Do Commie Crawlers like KL not recall the Declaration of Independence and why, or shall I say, how those who came here to what is now The United States of America? They left Government overreach and oppression. They left socialist and communist countries. Do Commie Crawlers like KL even know what is in The United States Constitution?

In fact, they do.

He does.

Think about this.

KL and other Commie Crawlers know exactly what they are doing. We can add Senator Dianne Feinstein to that Commie Crawler Swamp Monster group. She too was in the pool for U.S. Senate and she too is in support of socialized medicine[8], only she calls it "Universal Health Care," which by the way is Single Payer Health Care, the same thing as Government Controlled and Run Health Care. This is "socialism." Feinstein is also in support of aiding Illegal Aliens[9] in the name of, wait for it, "keeping families together." She is also for open border initiatives[10]. Not to mention, until later, the dozens of other initiatives she is for which would have our founders rolling in their graves.

Just wrong.

These issues just scratch the surface of what I found was wrong with all the Swamp Monsters running for the office of U. S. Senator in California.

Another obvious and crazy candidate who ran in California was the Little man, you can look him up. Little man is also a Commie Crawler. We call him the Little Commie Crawler.

With the Jungle Primary one never knows how the election will go. Hindsight is 20/20. Now we see him as a benign candidate, perhaps one thrown in to trip our candidacy up, but in its space in the Primary Election this candidate made even the most liberal of United States Citizens residing in the state of California scratch their head and say, "what is wrong with our countrymen!" The numbers didn't look good for him, but his Little Commie Crawler team made a big noise and unfortunately, or dare I say fortunately, in this case, the media was listening and reporting and the people did vote accordingly.

No one likes a hater.

Here is the kicker, which we saw happen in many cases nationwide in federal and state level races: Little Commie Crawler was a self-touted "MAGA," Make America Great Again candidate who states he supports President Trump.

You read that right.

He was banking on the Pro-Trump voters to believe him, just like another candidate we mention later on, only people were turned off by his Little Commie Crawler leanings. He is also a self-avowed Anti-Semite. LCC as we will call him, is said to be a Neo-Nazi[11].

This is no joke. The Little Commie Crawler ran on the Republican Ticket when his platform more closely falls within the realm of the hard-left Democrat Party platform.

Some people have fallen for the mantra about Neo-Nazi's being hard Right-Wing, this couldn't be further from the truth. Neo-Nazi's are in fact hard line Leftists.

People need to wake up to this truth. People also need to wake up and realize Progressives and Radicals are running on the Republican Tickets looking for automatic Republican, or name relatable votes to drain the platform and hand over the winning ticket to the Legitimate Leftist geared up and lined up for a big win.

Yes, it is tactical.

The Swamp is Deep, and it is real.

The Swamp is on both sides of the aisle. Many of these "Republicans" and "America First" candidates are blatantly lying or slanting the truth to have their way to bleed those votes. This is a national tactic. I have witnessed it. Here is the kicker about Little Commie Crawler, his platform is outright crazy and fanatical. While Little Commie Crawler called to put America First, he and his supporters clearly didn't want to put all Americans, United States Citizens, First -- only some of them. Those who they viewed as not deserving of any position in the United States were the Jews or those of Jewish descent – and others. Was there no limit to what they would do to rid America of the Jews, probably not?

In my case, I saw just how vile and toxic this particular candidate was first hand. Being that some of my family is of Jewish descent this candidate's supporters attacked my team and myself. The attacks were horrific written and verbal assaults on social media, on email, and even on phone calls. There is a slew of names I have now been called, which I never knew existed prior to running for United States Senate.

The Little Commie Crawler is the one candidate the California GOP had the guts to address at convention. They outright addressed the Little Commie Crawler and his Anti-Semite position, declining him entry to their State Convention[12].

Good. For. Them.

But… There were other "Republicans" who are not actually principled, party line and platform-based Republicans that the CA GOP didn't address and confront running on the Republican Party Platform who were at Convention.

Yes, they were let in, shared a table with another candidate,[13] and they attended the voting.

One particular candidate comes to mind, not even a Republican. A No Party Preference registered voter for years, who only registered as a Republican on March 9, 2018 to run for United States Senate on the Republican ticket, per an interview with a podcast and media platform called New Right Network.

This individual supports Medicare for All, including medical, dental, vision, and orthodontics – he calls it the whole body solution. Don't forget, this would be through a single payer system, government flow through. Socialism, about the furthest you could get from Republican Party value systems, in my view.

I digress. Let us get back to the foundational issue of party platform again.

Let's get an overview first. There seems to be a trend with Progressive Communist and Socialist politicians and candidates. Medicare for All, Universal Health Care, Single Payer Health Care all are now being added to the platform and an objective of those running within the Democratic Party. My position is clear on this issue. We have talked about "Medicare for All" being a Government Funded and a Government run Health Care system, which is Socialized Health Care, which is also the same as Universal Health Care.

This is socialism, a hop skip and a jump from full-blown communism, and government takeover of one of the largest industries in our nation. In our view, the Progressive and current

Democratic Party goal is to pass a full Government takeover of our Health Systems and Insurance Systems, sinking the capitalistic societal ship so far there is no option with massive taxpayer debt to the government, we as citizens now essentially work to fund the government, keeping our society afloat.

Presto – full circle, Communism.

No fear tactics here.

We are currently over twenty trillion dollars in debt. The tactic would not be too far off should these Progressive Democratic Party players attain such an objective. How can they accomplish this? Pay attention: by infiltrating the Republican Party. The party platform candidates are going unchecked not only by the Republican Party itself, but also by those who are within the party, including activists, radio hosts, analysts, and consultants.

Don't be fooled. Back to the "no big deal" socialist light, big government, climate change[14] proponent, radical environmentalist[15] mentality running on the Republican Party Platform. There was a "Republican," a person who just before the candidacy deadline closed decided to change their Party Affiliation to "Republican." After being a lifelong No Party Preference (NPP) Affiliation who voted any which way, even Democrat they did so to run for United States Senate on a "MAGA," "America First" platform on the Republican ticket.

This "Republican" was self-touted as wanting "Medicare for All," including medical, dental, vision and orthodontics[16]. In this case, this candidate is another Commie Crawler, though he is sneakier and corrupt in his approach to deception, so we call him a Slimy Slithering Sharpie.

Yes, another Swamp Monster.

Now, the aim isn't to just call folks names, no. The truth is harsh. We need to wake up and think about the tactics, think about the objectives in different format.

These people, Swamp Monsters, are actually liars or in their actions at the very least, and subsequently making them even worse, they are deceivers. Everything stated earlier is from the Slimy Slithering Sharpie's own SSS Monster mouth. Believer in Climate Change, Radical Environmentalist, Medicare for All, how is any of that wanting reduced regulation, smaller size and scope of government or looking to lower tax?

How does it meet the Republican Party Platform[17]?

It isn't. It doesn't.

Nonetheless, people hear what they want and see what they want through the lens of just don't care enough.

We need to care. We need to see.

We need to confront the issue of Swamp Monsters. First, we have to be able to identify them. Later we will talk about that more. In all honesty, all of this was pain staking to watch and, in our case, view individuals, namely those in leadership not addressing the Progressives in the room, literally.

Again.

And again.

And again.

There were more issues in the party, candidates running who were of notable concern in 2018.

The Chameleon types were rampant. How do they blend in? Manipulation of communication.

If you look like a duck, act like a duck, you are more than likely a duck. Sure, but when it comes to Swamp Monsters, many are crafty. Some Swamp Monsters may look like ducks and act like ducks, and you better duck!

They are in fact geese and will turn up in every area of the party organization to disrupt, tear apart, agitate in a way which appears like they are just waddling around like a duck knocking things over and you think, no big deal.

It is a big deal.

Mistake a goose for a duck and you will have a shock.

Geese have teeth and are inherently mean and territorial and will do what they have to accomplish their goal. In the case of these duck in disguise geese, Chameleon type Swamp Monsters, their goal isn't to help the party or the people, they want to destroy.

Many small destructive chips can go a long way.

One word: erosion.

One of the issues we face as a people and as a party is communication. The individual person, the spectrum of involvement within the Republican Party is notably vast. Many books have been written and research doled out in rolls about the subject, with no solutions and only more divisiveness added in.

What is currently being done isn't working.

It should also be noted that with the Party type positions there is a division built in, often on social issues, some Swamp Monsters also use faith or religion to divide, though they may make it appear they are uniting.

Always look to the fruit of their labor!

With that, let us look at the chameleon types, how the parties are grouped and how the swamp all fits together. Chameleon types play a large role in the divisiveness we see today. We don't call these Swamp Monsters Chameleons. Each one is notably distinct and different from another, for sure.

First, let us address the party.

Just as you have those in the Democratic Party who are further left leaning and Progressive and those who are more "centrist," the Republican Party has much of the same. Only in the case of the Republican Party there is less room for the "moderate" and "centrist" position when you get to the core of the Republican Party Platform.

It isn't that the platform is rigid; rather it is grounded in principles, value systems, and intertwines the social and fiscal aspects together with its embodiment being blanketed by a traditionalist outer core and perspective.

In fact, when you look at the Republican Party Platform it aligns itself within and under the United States Constitution.

Really, it looks to the founding basis of our Republic to guide the platform contents. Simply put, each piece of the Platform was put together carefully and strategically not to squash the United States Constitution but to clearly lay out the basis for why one might want to be a part of the party of "Yes."

It may seem bias of me to call the Republican Party Platform, the platform of "Yes," however I have looked at both platforms closely.

Anytime you release government from having a hold on the people it governs you free up those same people for opportunity, opportunity equates to "yes."

While we won't be covering the parties at length, I want to help lay out the basis by which you can see the swamp clearly on all sides. There are principles and lack of value systems, even totalitarian value systems within the Democratic Party Platform[18], which are in stark contrast to the Declaration of Independence and the United States Constitution.

Throw these contrasts to the real world, into real life interactions of the people they play out as what we see in real time, division.

In the platform of diversity and affirmative action, these positions on their own are in conflict within the Democrat Party, dividing their membership from those in the real world who view things different from them. Another example is Diversity and Affirmative Action, which are supposed to encourage inclusiveness, yet the true aim is far more sinister. Other areas where the Democratic Party Platform is fueling the fire of division, look at Identity Politics, Political Correctness, Religion and so many more we will talk about later.

Topically, looking at both major parties, one can see why the nation is polarized. We have two growing factions who couldn't be further apart from one another, and both of which seem to include people who are moving away from the United States Constitution. It seems.

To clarify, those Swamp Monsters in the Republican Party are undermining the Party platform shifting the perspective to a position where people are meant to perceive the Republican Party [Platform] is changing.

It isn't, the Party is being infiltrated.

The Platform is strong.

In short, the people are too trusting and their entire United States Constitution supporting platform is being eroded.

We need to expose the Swamp and Swamp Monsters on both sides, all sides, really. Those people putting United States Citizens last and their agenda first and running over the United States and California Constitution in the process need exposed every opportunity possible.

To expose them you need to become familiar. You need to understand the Swamp before you can understand the creatures within it.

The Swamp encompasses the entire nation. California, where I reside is huge. Largely comprised of a deep and thick Swamp, primarily on the coastal side, California is crawling with all sorts. And as we mentioned earlier there are those Chameleon type swamp monsters and others encroaching on the even driest of areas. Swamp Monsters adapt and evolve.

We have learned that over the last few years in spades.

The nation is vast.

Even where there are moral and ethical communities, conservative communities, those areas where cities are operational and functional with minimal government intrusion and citizens largely reside independently, keep an eye out!

The swamp isn't always imbedded and seeping into all areas is it?

Again, be aware.

There are areas where the landscape is less swampy, but even when this is the case there is likely an infestation somewhere of the Swamp Monsters.

Look at Iowa. Iowa is currently being infiltrated by all kinds of swamp monsters, even some like the Swampiest of the Swampers.

Back to the California Swampland varieties. When you have a Swamp Monster who is like a chameleon. He has a mission in an environment, the climate, the creatures around him, those he needs to blend in with or he will be tossed out of the territory! That is right. If it is discovered in an environment there is someone who isn't what they profess to be, people will fight back against the Swamp Monster.

The key: blend, blend, blend.

Why the big lead in?

Well, it is for two particular "Republicans" running on our party platform in 2018 who need addressing.

One Swamp Monster is a candidate for U.S. Senate, a sneaky one. Something with this person was not right, not at all. We will call him the Wall Climbing Weasel. I am sure you are thinking, "Weasels in the Swamp?"

YES!

Weasels are highly adaptable, they even change their outer self to blend in. Yes, their fur. No joke. In all seriousness though, back to the real life Swampers. The Sneaky Wall Climbing Weasel over time was able to get his boogle[19] into the fold as well.

At first glance, my position was to hold our clean race and run the straight and narrow. Naturally. But there was this weasel, or "duck" who was principled, so it seemed, of high moral standard, and would stick to the issues as other actual "ducks" were.

Great.

Mmmm, it didn't turn out that way.

We learned this Sneaky Wall Climbing Weasel was using liberal and corrupted tactics to gain political favor amongst good, unknowing people.

Not only did he court good folks to seemingly earn their trust, in many cases people came to me concerned, asking me questions only to be upset by the truth.

Just wrong.

Over time, the discovery of the Wall Climbing Weasel spreading inaccurate information, it became more apparent. It just kept building. Even worse, it was told to us he was using intimidation tactics with potential constituents and supporters, publicly promoting and using misogyny to alienate folks, and until I looked close enough, I couldn't see it. In point of fact, he was using a type of gentrification tactical maneuver to juxtaposition then divide our party in the name of faith and religion.

Appalling. Outrage.

All of this is traditionally speaking, un-Republican. Extremely immoral and unethical, all of it.

Just wrong.

Can people be so blinded? When desperate, yes, they will look through that lens of just don't care enough, rush in, and go for it no matter the cost.

The hallmark of Republicans, Ronald Reagan, saw many things as an actor in Hollywood, then as Governor and President. Pushing through, he held tight to the traditional all-American values Republicans hold dear.

How do you want to be known by others especially as it relates to your family and your faith-based values? This is important. America has a much higher percentage of faith-based citizens than the mainstream media would like you to know about. Even Wikipedia shares that encompassing all faith-based persons in the United States, we are around 77%[20]. Those who profess to be Christian in the United States is about 71%, respectively. Republican numbers relating to faith are much higher.

The Religious Right as some call it, or Christian Right largely associates with and vote in line with the Republican Party, as do Evangelicals. Conservatives, Republicans are largely faith-based as a whole.

The same is true, especially those running for elected office, those who are currently holding leadership positions, there seems to be an outward inflation of their faith.

Why do I say this? There are those who I have met along the congressional path who clearly love God, profess Jesus Christ is their Lord and Savior, even that they are not ashamed to declare they are a Christian and their faith is a large part of who they are, this is an attempt to display the foundation of their belief systems.

The majority of those I have met are in fact genuine, more often than not you can see the display of their faith in their everyday interactions and approach to politics, addressing the issues on the table, conflicts, and how they operate their campaigns. And there are those who are not genuine, those who are, I am sure, Christians, but they are using their faith as a heavy stick to sway votes and support.

How can you tell?

Well, the way by which those who profess to be Christian and go after the faith-based vote, which is tactical over being a witness of their faith.

This approach doesn't just apply to faith-based vote getting; you can see their artificial approach as they go after all votes actually. Their overall approach to their campaigns and the way they operate minute to minute seems to be inconsistent with their respective faith.

This was the case with the Wall Climbing Weasel.

I have never witnessed someone use God and everything we as Christians and as people of faith hold sacred to tear another apart in the way he did, and publicly. In addition, the whole "I am more Christian approach" than Erin Cruz was definitely disturbing when I witnessed it from afar at an event I attended. It really woke me up to how far people will go to buy a vote. Selling their souls to greed, ego, and for personal gain.

It saddened me to see someone would deceive others. I'm not sure it's something I ever wanted to witness, manipulation using religion.

Many of you laugh, we do have it on the Earth, I am not inept.

Yes, I know, I have seen it on the television, but in real life this was difficult to palate.

Praise be to God those individuals he was speaking to were solid

Christians who were not fooled or swayed, and in fact, met him with patience and blunt truth about what approach he was taking and why it was wrong. I will share with you part of the story.

Who is he? Who he says he is and who he actually is are two very different things.

Like a Weasel, their coats change with their surroundings. They adapt and blend, though they are still the same creature. He is a sneaky, cynical man who smiles often, yet you can see the dark overture playing in the back of his mind, in his soul, by looking into his beady cold eyes. The tension in his face and neck, the grip of his hands, the way his clothes are put together, there is a costuming going on.

Complete lack of authenticity, unfortunately.

I met the Weasel in northern California. He approached me with clear intentions, to insult, intimidate, and cause nothing but division and trouble.

There was a stench, figuratively speaking.

This is the exact opposite of what we need.

He first approached me outdoors whilst I was attending an event at the State Capitol. I knew there were several candidates for U.S. Senate at the event, though I had no intention to interact on that level with any of them except where appropriate to encourage civic interaction by the people involved.

As I was networking, a tiny man approached me in a stiff blue suit. It first appeared I needed to make myself available for conversation, and then I looked down at his hands. His hands were clutching marketing materials nervously. As I looked up and expressed my willingness to engage in conversation, his nerves quieted. His demeanor shifted into an ominously confrontational stance. So obvious it was uncomfortable.

I took a deep breath.

This tiny Weasel of a man moved from being at a professional and conversational distance to clearly asserting himself (and his insecurities) by moving too close, showing no respect, no personal or professional space. He went on to share he had been in business over 40 years. "Wow," I thought. Observing what I had over the first 3 minutes, this statement couldn't portray any good thing.

In fact, where many other people stand, I would be inclined to say if they expressed being in business 40 years this would be an impressive, wonderful thing, an accomplishment.

In this Swamp Monster's case, the Weasel was posturing, fluffing, in an attempt to gain ground.

Highly unflattering.

You have probably met smart and accomplished people. It is an utter delight to hear of their journeys. We can learn so much from others.

Over my career and years of political activism, I have met so many accomplished professionals—be it in academia or in their respective trades.

Don't measure the man by his wallet or title.

There are those who have literally transformed the world in which we live and those who make an impact with what they do as a natural result. The majority of brilliant minds, world wonders and brainiacs of humankind, those of whom I can do nothing more than to glean insight into what they have done and take their wisdom and advice for the betterment of who I am. I often think, "How we can grow the world together?"

A brilliant and talented mind must not be wasted, even if your experience is to be the one who comes in contact, not necessarily the one with the mind!

Embrace your ability to connect with others and grow, grow, grow.

Weasels of the world, I have learned they are takers, not actually givers and growers.

Be aware and grow your knowledge of what each looks like!

On to what happened with this Swamp Monster. Part way

through the campaign cycle the Wall Climbing Weasel came to my hometown. It was clear over a period of time, he had been stalking our event listings, a tactic which is not uncommon in campaigning. They call it "riding on the coat tails of another," essentially letting someone else pave an easier path.

Truth be told I am a Trail Blazer at heart and a warrior who is not easily distracted, not one to "ride coat tails" for the ease of life path.

It was incredibly frustrating to see people who call themselves "leaders" and "reformers," looking for people to trust them, ride on the coat tail path of someone else due to laziness.

Several times the Wall Climbing Weasel imbedded himself in events I was scheduled to attend, then showing up at my hometown, appearing at an open forum was not happenstance. There are 39 Million people in California and 58 counties.

California is YUGE.

Despite Wall Climbing Weasel not aggressively campaigning he would show up at select events where I was. I had traveled up and down the state many times. Attending dozens of forums where other candidates would share their positions, their platforms, answering questions of the potential constituents, this was nothing new.

I love a good, strong, energized event!

This particular instance of him showing up was different.

It was.

Very.

I knew it would be different, and I was right. This would not be the first event I had attended with the Wall Climbing Weasel. As I mentioned before he was popping up. It was only a matter of time before it would get nasty. I could tell he was not who he was portraying to others, unfortunately.

This event was a gathering I was looking forward to. I knew there would be people attending who had been looking forward to meeting me and talking about the future of California. For them, it turned out to be upsetting to see people treat others with such disrespect.

What happened? I will tell you.

A few weeks prior to the event in my hometown I was approached by a person who I knew was not in to the U.S. Senate race to find a strong candidate to win. This person was pleasant but not an alliance or a friend. There were obvious intentions, which at that time were not clear. He approached me at another event in the same region as my hometown inviting me to a forum. He was clearly nervous. His plan was a go and soon I would see just how manipulative even the "nicest" guy who is well liked could be. Sure, he can be nice. Can be.

Understand, in politics you can't take things personally. While we build lifelong alliances, friendships even, there are still interactions, which are all business. Remaining objective is essential.

So, this man, it turns out he is part of Wall Climbing Weasel's boogle.

Yup. You heard me right!

After arriving to the event in my hometown, the cordial forum turned murky swamp so quickly it was like a sudden storm rolled in.

The sky got thick, the rain poured into the swamp making a turn up of sludge and muck appear and causing a drag in time, making an uncomfortable energy affecting those unknowing folks in the room.

I entered the door way, walking into the large hall filled with good folks wanting to hear local and state-wide candidates. And then it happened, I looked up and saw familiar faces, ushering me over to sit with them at the usual spots at the table. Most folks in my region knew I was traveling and working anywhere from 18-20-hour days and in this case, I had already driven a half a day to attend this event from another region in the north.

Tired and excited to see my fellow Republican women and men, I settled in to my seat after saying hello and greeting a few familiar faces.

The weight and posturing from the other side of the room was heavy. You could feel the heat of the eyes and judgments from afar. It felt like pure evil and in that minute, in an instant, the movement and the productivity in the room became slow and messy.

Very messy.

Have you ever watched a zombie show? They walk and drag, this was it – zombies in the real world.

I was called up to speak.

Turning on my mic I started my talk.

This talk was following a day where immigration, human trafficking and other hard topics were in the news. My goal was to talk about the tough solutions we need so badly in California and in the United States Senate. Rarely do I stammer, but in this case, there was a shuffling from a certain table and there was a level of disrespect and agitating happening in the room.

Yes. Full-grown men acting like boys in a schoolyard.

If I were a man, they wouldn't have dared.

It is true. Not because all men carry on like that, only some.

Childish as it was, I pressed on delivering my talk and so as it were there was evidence my talk made a strong impact. Thank God!

It was after my talk, while canvassing the room and watching the interactions of the people, the confirmation came. Indeed, the man who invited me to the event was part of the Wall Climbing Weasel's boogle. Not only did they sit together, they carried on like the twins in the movie hit Alice in Wonderland.

It was repulsive.

Why repulsive?

Because they were up to no good and unashamed, they carried on.

And then it happened.

Even worse than the displays of boyhood schemes and disrespect, there was a talk given which was enough to push a fellow patriot and countryman to call the Wall Climbing Weasel on the carpet.

The Weasel delivered the most grandiose speech claiming he made thousands and thousands of jobs. He went on and on about what innovation he had done in his life, which in all honestly if it were true who would knock a man for being highly successful, providing jobs, and impacting their community? That is a great thing, *if it were true*.

There is an issue though. Weeks before he delivered a speech in a small room of 100 people where he said something much different.

We need to know the truth.

Which was the lie?

Did he "create" thousands of jobs or was the truth reflected in the other statement he made just a few weeks prior?

You see, he made somewhat of a moving speech just weeks

before where he stated he hadn't been highly successful and didn't have much in the way of job creation or in accomplishments – he employed some people.

I have both speeches on record. To listen, it baffles me.

The speech this weasel made weeks before was in fact compelling and far more believable, especially where his delivery was concerned.

This raised my brow about his positions when in this more recent town hall he went grandiose. Whichever is true is what the people need to hear. The people have been so cheated by their "representation," they deserve to be addressed honestly so they can make an assessment and decide how they will cast their vote.

Is honesty too much to ask?

The truth may not always be glamorous, but is holds great value, something that can't be bought or manipulated. When someone attempts to manipulate truth it only exposes who they are, it can never change the facts within that the truth or pervert the reality at hand.

There are several issues I have with the above statement the Wall Climbing Weasel had to say. He was talking about building and innovating. Self-stated, he is supposedly good at this, if he can remember the truth and share the real version of what his life has been, of course.

This grandstanding was like an actor on a stage, I as another potential constituent was not only turned off, I was flat out disgusted. By this point, he realized folks in the "Den of Thieves" were not sharing all information they were receiving. They were actually helping to share misinformation, which was unfortunate.

This is exactly where our news outlets are failing America and California. Had the news outlets been in each of these rooms and reporting on the topics, the candidates, and the platforms they could have exposed the lies and manipulation of Californians statewide by charlatans like the Wall Climbing Weasel.

We need to play a stronger role in our ability to share information within the Republican Party as a whole. Back to the issue.

Facts not fakedom.

Building and innovating, both are great in business.

In government, I really do not want them expanding anything (except our levels of freedom, restoring liberty, back to days of old) and especially creating a larger government. The bloat we have now is beyond what we should have, and government is not efficient at anything. The entire role of Government is distorted in today's America. Government has reached outside its role. My view on government is this: Government is meant to govern for stability and order only.

Government's role is not to legislate every area of our lives.

Legislation should be to protect and defend those who reside here. As an example, gun laws should exist in an event a person commits a crime so the criminal can be charged and held responsible. Gun laws should not impede on a lawful citizen's right to have or bear arms.

Stay out of my house.

Stay out of my pocket book, and don't legislate my life and liberties away.

When someone like Weasel the Wall Climber says things like he has, it is a huge concern and it begs the question, "What circus act is he playing today?"

Certainly, the speech given was from a position of someone who shouldn't be running for high office. In fact, the context of the speech gave thought to which race he was running for because the roles he was discussing were not roles one would be doing as a United States Senator.

To those out there reading this about he said she said it is extremely simple. The founders had it right.

We need limited government, in order to get back to that space we now need to limit government.

Back to Wall Climbing Weasel's speech.

He kept saying he would create jobs.

Note to the Weasel.... Government isn't in the business of "creating jobs," except under Obama where we saw federal and state government job creation at an all-time high. Big government breeds and you get more big government.

Government isn't in the corporate job creation business at all; it does a far better job at killing jobs by default of what it is: money bleeder.

In order for jobs to flourish, pre-tax aka regulation, should be cut. Overall taxation should be lowered, tax law simplified, red tape needs cut. Government should be in the business of getting out of the way of business by doing just that, keeping regulations low, tax low, and allowing for strong operations by ensuring the nation has strong national security so our countrymen can flourish at what they do best: creation and innovation.

This flaunting of the Wall Climbing Weasel's lack of knowledge about business vs government was stifling, though as bothersome as it was, it didn't really top the cake.

The topping of the cake was far worse.

All saw it. A disturbing display of political posturing, dirty words, and outright disgusting displays of misogyny marked by societal and gender gentrification. That is being gentle about it. Before the weasel spoke, the room was light, airy, even with the attitudes of the boogle, grumbling, and the like.

And then it happened.

As he started to speak it was as if dark stormy clouds rolled in, thunder, a heaviness was about.

The air in the room changed.

Could I be the only one sensing this?

No, I don't think so.

It wasn't just the words. It wasn't just the mannerisms; it was the tone, the cockiness in his character.

The entire speech was filled with "the men," "the men," "the men," type perspective.

There are many recordings found online where people in attendance archived and shared the event talks. What was really said, to this day, disturbs me, especially given those who are fooled by this Swamp Monster.

In his political punches and jabs at me, those in the room got highly uncomfortable and given it was a forum, naturally I would be allotted a moment to respond or address these grotesque jabs.

Thank goodness.

As the weasel sat down, the people in the room were looking at me, readily awaiting my response. Not a moment passed, they were eager!

Just as I maneuvered to request a moment to address the crowd, I see a friendly face rise to the floor. Up the podium went the brightest sweetest woman. Phew!

Then it happened.

A statement is made by the Angel of Light,[21] stepping in as if to glide down from the clouds on high, Angel of Light says in good sport to the crowd, "We will hear and allow a short response from…"

And an interruption ensued.

There was a rebuttal to the President of the Club's assertion to process. They moved to say, against the President, this wasn't ok!

Why? Because it wasn't a debate, rebuttal wasn't proper.

The Angel of Light gracefully and assertively stood her ground, stating it wasn't a debate, it was a public forum where we politely will hear from candidates about their platforms and positions.

Given I was not able to refute what was said, it was only appropriate I be given a moment to respond.

Way to lead!

So, after a few minutes and Club President's address to the people I stood up and addressed the crowd and went to bat about the position of those in representation roles. I stayed mindful to those in attendance and their desire to have addressed the issues which matter to them, their families and communities. Immediately after my response, the negativity ruminated from the boogle.

The Wall Climbing Weasel was highly agitated, waving his arm and abruptly and rudely shaking his head stating he wanted to respond.

Why!

Had there been no jabs at me or my platform and stances or my background there would have been no reason for me to address the sneaking and manipulative jabs.

Why not just present your case, how you plan to solve issues, and highlight your platform?

Ego, that is why.

We have enough egos in elected office. We don't need more.

Angel denied his request only to have the Weasel rudely interject.

No class.

No respect.

None.

All of this spoke multitudes to the crowd about his lack of decorum and lack of respect for the leadership and people present.

Would they see it that way?

It was then I looked around seeing the people's response in the hall and their complete lack of respect for the Weasel.

Thank goodness for good minded and principled people.

Cool heads prevail.

The meeting shifted and there was an introduction given to another candidate, one for whom I hold great respect. He is a true Swamp Buster.

Justice J is a true fighter, someone who can be trusted to provide perspective and insight. There will come a time to talk about this fighter. Now is not that time.

Where the Weasel is concerned, Justice was served. This reaffirms we have a great deal of work to do as people. The good, strong, and just must get involved and stay involved.

There are so many areas where we as principled citizens of this nation can make impact. We must not allow those around us to play a power role in the goals we set forth for ourselves, impacting those we are working with.

Retain your power in the situation.

How do you do that? There are ways. In many cases observing plays a large role in the decision making for action. Read on for more information on weapons and tactics.

We find there is equilibrium in the operation of human interaction. There is only so long an inauthentic person can fool those around them.

In Weasel's case, he was swiftly dealt with that day. Justice met him face to face in more ways than one. The unfortunate thing where the Weasel is concerned is there are so many people desperate for help and solutions. He reminds me of the traveling salesmen of old with tonics laced with nothing more than fragrance and flavoring, not offering any cure, preying on those needing the most help and abusing their vulnerable state. In doing so, the Weasel did, and continues to do this, literally in the name of religion and Jesus.

My heart aches when I write this. As I said earlier, thinking someone would do this was beyond comprehension, and to see others help him it was heart breaking.

They were fooled.

Even Christians fell for the sham.

We must do our homework and not follow blindly, folks. Not even the most trusted resource is exempt from good intentions and the ability to be manipulated and fooled, or at worst, they could be corrupted.

Stay eyes wide open.

When you think your eyes are open, blink just to be sure.

Pinch yourself, if you must.

Stay eyes wide open.

Just when you meet someone who you see as possibly meeting your expectations and then you realize their actions, their intentions, they are not of good moral standing. Follow your intuition, your instincts. Stand on your trust in God. Have faith in Him and yourself. Look to where He has brought you from, where He wants to take you in your life. Stay focused on your charge in life, in this journey, in your journey. Focus. More often than not, true realities of the situation will reveal themselves, always.

At this point in the campaign, the boundaries of what I thought were possible to attain with my determination, they were being pushed to the outer limits. I was determined to go where God wanted to take me, if not for myself, I would do so for the people, for Him. The truth was in front of me.

Unlock the door, let go of the knob and let God move.

This is exactly what I did.

The swamp is deep in the United States of America. The Swamp is a sewer in California. Not only is it deep, it is thick and morbid, filled with all kinds of creatures from all over the earth, those who belong and those who don't.

Tread lightly, but with purpose or you seriously could get swallowed up and be infected by some of the contagions here.

There is one last notable Swamp Monster we will talk about, for now. He was the opposite of the Wall Climbing Weasel, yet he still is a Swamp Monster. At times, it is hard to tell which is worse.

Is there a worse though, really?

Both are bad.

Both are dangerous.

Both are not a productive use of energy to better the California Republic or the United States of America.

Both wasted the energy of the California Citizenry.

Both frauded people by their interactions and led people to believe their intentions were good and proper.

Both bled the vote.

The only difference besides the genus they belong to as Swamp Monsters, one bled the vote twice.

There is a creature within the Swamp who many call a RINO. RINO is an Acronym that stands for Republican In Name Only. Some bonafide Republicans say it is un-Republican to judge others in the party for their actions, and saying one is a RINO is big "no-no."

Well, I believe our hand is forced, *we must look at the realities of today.* The realities of right now, and for many years as of late, we have folks who are not Republicans in our Party.

Our Party is increasingly being infiltrated and weakened by those who want to see their own visions met. I give emphasis to increasingly because we have been infiltrated for some time.

This is not a new trend. There is an exponential increase in non-Republicans in the Republican Party. People in the Party, those who want to stay hush and not talk about the issues that need addressing are not just a part of the problem; they are the problem.

Many in Republican circles know the candidate I am going to talk about. Many like him. It isn't that I like him or don't. That is neither here nor there. People need to pull back and be objective.

Think about it from another angle.

When we go to the doctor, we may not want to hear what he has to say or want to have surgery if we need one. The doctor is there to do a job, to help you, and you pay him for his services. We don't have to "like" him we need him to do his job.

Politicians are the same way.

We need doers, action takers, visionaries, and true leaders. We don't need those who are trying to undermine the entire body. We don't need or want those who work against those actually working to better our situation. We need just the opposite. We need those who want better, not just those in the Party, but for everyone.

In the case of many RINOs they may in fact ascribe to the Republican Party Platform, only their intentions are contrary to actually accomplishing the goals of the same party to which they belong, effectively undermining everything the people are working so hard to accomplish.

So, by all their beliefs, their perspectives, they still are RINOs because two wrongs, they don't make a right.

Being a Republican, then working against the Republicans is as un-Republican as one can get.

There was a candidate, someone I looked closely at prior to running for office. Naturally anyone would examine what candidates are in the pool prior to making a run for high office. It was important to me not to be what I mentioned above, a vote bleeder. There were so many people running for U.S. Senate in 2018, it was like overloaded tinsel on a Christmas Tree.

Glaring out your eyes you have to look close to make sure you are seeing what you are and clear about what action you want to take.

Yes, tinsel.

There was in the vast herd, a Mini White RINO.

His name? Tricky Tozer. He was very, very tricky. For those who love definitions, tricky means to be "deceitful or crafty.[22]"

His demeanor? Unassuming.

He is like Mr. Cellophane.

You might not notice him when he is around. Normally this might not be an issue with an election for a public official except this is for a U.S. Senate seat for the state of California, the largest economy in the nation and the 5th largest economy in the world. We need strong proponents who will represent a diverse state in Washington D.C.

Among Tricky Tozer's inability to articulate the issues, have a strong voice, and represent a diverse state there was a larger issue. In 2016 there was also a large pool of candidates who ran for U.S. Senate in California for the newly vacated seat of Barbara Boxer (D). Tricky Tozer was one of them.

Many folks may not know, but the 2016 race for United States Senate was one for the books. On the Republican Ticket there were *two candidates* who are former heads of the California Republican Party. Both candidates were marked to take a large chunk of the vote. In a large pool of candidates this is highly problematic, especially due to the "Jungle Primary" system in California.

A jungle is right.

A jungle in a Swamp!

Fitting.

What is a jungle primary? In many states you have party primary where each party has registrants, those registrants vote in their respective races for their party putting up the top candidate for the general election. The two top vote getters from the winning top two parties go head to head in the General Election. That would mean if the Republican and Democratic Party had the most voters casting for their respective wins, these two parties would send their winner to the top for a dual at the ballot box!

In California this isn't the case. In earlier years (2010[23]) the voters voted in favor of Prop 14, a measure to throw the party system out the window.

Now as it stands the top two vote getters overall in the Primary Election advance to the General Election, regardless of party affiliation. As a result, understanding what is at stake, how can two CRP leaders well versed in politics rightfully run against one another in a packed pool of swampers?

It is beyond comprehension. Or is it?

Now, there are more Swamp Monsters involved in this triangle love affair of bleeding the vote away from the people of the Republican Party and toward the Democratic Party. We will talk about these swampers a bit later.

There it is, these two top dogs will split the heavy hitter vote of the Republican Party and then there are a few more Republican

"Loyalists" running in the wings.

One of them is Tricky Tozer.

Who is Tricky Tozer? He is a person who is active in the Republican Party and bled an additional 1% of the vote away from the two top dogs.

This is enough for me to not be able to support his run for U.S. Senate in 2018.

If you see two top dogs are running for office and are not working to help narrow the vote and ensure a strong top two presence, there is an issue with your motives.

If you only garner 1% of the vote, bled a prior vote, and are running again, there is a fundamental issue with your reasoning for running for office.

Not dropping out with two top hitters in points to an ego issue.

Tricky Tozer decided to run again for United States Senate in 2018. After reviewing the historical information there was no way I could support his bid. This is someone who has more self interest in running than seeing the big picture needs of the Citizens residing in California.

Move over ego, we have no room for you.

It wouldn't be until much later when it became so clear I was right.

Boy am I glad I decided to run for United States Senate. This swamper Tozer is exposed! There are many factual and evidence-based instances of swamper activity by this Sneaky Tricky Tozer. We will go over the swampers swampy playground later.

Know I don't take this lightly or just in play to call him what I do. There is evidence! There is a boogle of Tozer's own ilk to be talked about .at length.

What is worse, a progressive Democrat who states his case or a "Republican" who is playing games with their own ticket, readily handing over the ticket to the Democrats via foul political play?

The RINO is worse.

Quite frankly, knowing what I know it couldn't have been better, my run for United States Senate. Not only did I have the Democratic Party against me, I had the RINO wing of the Republican Party against my team and run for office as well.

A badge of honor.

Our teams fought hard and we continue forward to help in the battle to restore conservatism to the Republican Party. We stand strong! We stand together!

Rolling back to when my friend asked me, "Who are you going to vote for against Dianne Feinstein?" My answer was I don't know.

When she suggested I run for office, I thought – I better pray about this! It was at that point when I looked at that pool, near 30 people, cough-cough, swamp.

There was no way with current California corruption and politics I could vote for those on the ticket.

There you have it, both feet in we go, if the People want it.

I declared my test the waters campaign.

When you think about it, who better to run for office than someone you can trust, someone you know who will protect and defend the United States Constitution, someone the people can count on?

When that person is you, it is surreal.

Truly, I didn't see it in myself until my friend pointed it out. Only a hand full of days passed and people wanted an "all in" candidate, someone they knew would not back down from the corruption, from the thugs of the Democrat Party, from those in the GOP they didn't trust.

I answered the call. If we are to serve the public we must listen to their needs and be there, observe, assess, and take action.

Erin Cruz for US Senate was formed.

Behind the scenes and unknown to me at the time, this is when the swamp busters were being formed; only we didn't call it that. What was their charge? Their charge was to expose the Commie Crawlers and Swamp Monsters plaguing California.

CHAPTER THREE
COLLISION OF COLUSION & COMMIE CRAWLERS

Governor Jerry Brown, Senator Dianne Feinstein and so many others in elected office are loathed here in California by a strong amount of Republicans. Why? Because of their infringing policies on liberty and freedom of the People of California.

When I decided to run for public office, first announcing my test the waters campaign, I thought surely much of what the President at the time was talking about was exaggerated. Many things coming out of the White House in the President's tweets about collusion, the deep state, Russia, bots, election tampering and obstruction seemed far-fetched even by my open-minded standards.

As soon as I launched my campaign the people were reaching out, there were needs that were not being met by government officials, there were reports those around me were indeed looking to get out about the issues we were facing and a great deal in some way reflected on the very things President Trump was working so hard to communicate to the people.

I found out really quickly the media both liberal and conservative were not our friends and the deep state was in fact a reality.

As we progressed through the campaign cycle, gaining ground as I traveled the state there were very few in the media willing to cover our campaign, the people's campaign.

The first big box media outlet to cover our campaign was a local channel, NBC. Overall, they were gracious giving a 30-minute interview to share about our platform and our progress. I thought they were at least accommodating until it came to their report.

What was it like?

Well, the reporter was late.

Only then to make it clear she would interview and put the piece together later in the day. We know what that means.

Media should be reporting to the people, sharing information. Give the people options. Freedom of the Press gives the media the ability to have access to information to provide to the populous for the specific goal of retention of Liberty and Freedom.

Where our current media is standing, they stand on the side of profits, clicks and serving a specific agenda.

The story ran two times about my candidacy. It was remarkable the response I received. You see, that slimy swamp dweller, the progressive agendist presenter, she threw me under the bus.

Don't worry she only ran over me and backed up and ran over me again.

Her closing comments are what drove people to respond to me and reach out. "If you can run, anyone can."

Intended as a derogatory comment and negative thing the people were on fire about how rude she was and how they were thrilled a regular person who cared about the people and the nation was running for office and brave enough to stand up against the machine.

WOW!

I received one letter from a gal who said she will never watch that station again, remarking her whole family will be voting for me and they are not even Republicans. Yes!

Note after note arrived on social media and it was clear, bad press is great press and the people saw right through what big box media was trying to do. What a relief.

I now knew exactly how President Trump felt, and in my case, this was just a narrow view of the bias media. There were many lessons learned about how exactly media was not working on behalf of the people from the perspective of my campaign, our campaign. They, meaning media, seem to work against the needs of the people in many cases, unless it suits them by feeding division and fueling hot topics and news.

Brass Tax: Big Box Media does not want solutions.

There is zero financial benefit in offering information, true options for solutions to the problems of today. Media and news outlets only make money when there is conflict, division, and chaos as it seems. It is in media's best interest to keep the drama going to keep growing their pocket books.

Drama equals clicks.

Clicks equal money.

As a side note, if media covers a candidate they are giving "free advertising." Why do that when there are million-dollar campaigns like those of Feinstein and others who are willing and ready to sign multimillion-dollar advertising campaigns during an election year?

Media and news outlets are a public service?

Only when it pays. Even, or should I say, especially if they are government funded or subsidized.

That is not what the Founders were securing when they addressed freedom of the press. The founders were protecting you, me, bloggers, small agencies -- all of our rights to get out information to the people! What we see today in "media" is a bastardization and complete abuse of their power. There should be distinct lines drawn in what constitutes those organizations categorized as "press." In the case of the everyday citizen, podcasts, new media and other grass root outlets, they lend to be more reliable even through a filter of an armature with bias.

The "big box" giants package and use complex architecture when filtering the information, they put out often giving it such an angle of belief they can construct believable stories using completely twisted material. This is an absolute shame.

Getting back to the basics, the Founders left our Constitution broad and simplistic for a reason. For example, why should a person or small group not be let to gather information and start up a new press agency? Why, if we are all created equal should one person have more access to information about our communities and government than another.

How could we possibly defeat corruption unless there is complete and total access to information and freedom of the press? Every day citizens should be involved. This should be encouraged. Should you or I be stopped from speaking freely and having the ability to report information the people need to operate as a free society? Absolutely not.

Where is the issue? There are those organizations who are given full access to information and they abuse their power not for solutions rather for position, division, and profit.

Is profit bad? No, it is not.

It remains though, that such outlets are manipulating the general public, unequally meeting their duty to be considered free press. They report on politics, on those in elected office, but they are not required to offer a solution of a candidate when they report on that news. For example, if Politician Jan is in office, she is running for re-election and the news agency reports on her actions in office, should they be required to consult the individual campaigning against her? Think on that.

The purpose of free press is to inform the public.

The United States Constitution is clear; the Bill of Rights is crystal clear. It states the following in the Bill of Rights, Amendment I: "Congress shall make no law respecting an establishment of religion or prohibiting the free exercise thereof; or abridging the freedom of speech, or of the press; or the right of the people peaceably to assemble, and to petition the government for a redress of grievances.[24]"

It is simple. There are those who understand the Founding Father's vision and those who do not. Of those who understand the Founding Father's vision, there are those who support them and those who do not. Individuals who do not understand the Founding Father's vision need to look at the Declaration of Independence, the United States Constitution, and the Bill of Rights, taking it all in at its most simplistic form.

Back to the big box media outlet who had me on their outlet, there is one thing to be said. In any news organization we must remember it is comprised of people, employees. Those employees may or may not be in alignment with the agency itself. As in any corporation there will be great employees and not so great folks working there. One of the highlights at the news agency was a cameraman on staff. Now, I don't know if he agreed with me or not, supported me or not, was a "D" or an "R" or an "I," and frankly to me it did not matter. He was an absolute professional and someone who was objective in that he was clearly remaining neutral, doing his job. His professionalism put me more at ease than the Swamp Monster who interviewed me. Clearly, I do best with regular down-to-earth people over those with egos and agendas!

In short: the cameraman – He ROCKED!

This media interaction ordeal throughout the campaign was going to be an uphill battle, especially after being run over and then having the bus back up and run over me again.

There was one media outlet, which proved to appear to want to share information with the people, and conservatives. This was OANN.

Their entire outlet pushed to provide information to the people, a job well done. Their teams were not only professional they were engaged with the people of this state.

It would be nice if other so called "conservative" or "free press" news outlets were of the same caliber. I don't come from the position of bias, simply put, if these outlets do their job we would be in a much better position as a state and as a nation. OANN had me on their network and on a show they produce more than once, not always as a candidate.

The people within our communities need our help. They need insight from folks who care and want to make a difference, is it not what media is to do?

Isn't media supposed to better the world through information?

Not one for creating headlines with stunts and wanting to get down to work with Californians, we would need to find a different approach, a better way.

That we did.

CHAPTER FOUR
SWAMP BUSTERS

We kicked off the test the waters campaign. Would the people step up? Would they want me to run for elected office? If I ran for office, it would have to be a "God thing." Everyone knows you can't run for high office alone. In a state with 39 million people we would have to have expansive support to be successful and make impact.

I certainly wouldn't have people thrown money into a campaign unless we were going to go all the way, fighting, and not backing down.

Just a short time into the test the waters campaign, money was pouring in, but the people did want to know I was in it for the win, I was in is for the fight. This was not a win for me or a fight for me, they wanted to know I was going to stand tall and strong for them, representing them and their voice no matter what.

It was at that point when I did jump all in and called on people to step up and volunteer. When I first launched the formal campaign people literally laughed at me, at our little team. Literally. Who were the swamp monsters doing this? Mostly Republicans. I was shocked. There were those who said we were doing things all wrong. What was my message to the haters? Well, honey, if you think I am doing things all wrong, offer a hand, volunteer and help out. Correct. For nearly 2/3rds of a decade Democrats have held the California U.S. Senate Seat. Critique me? Why? Was it intimidation, friction, division, ego issues, perhaps insecurity? I believe it to be raw fear.

Those actors in the party didn't fear me, they fear what I represent. Only those true to the United States Constitution in raw form were brave enough to stand with me, proud and not intimidated. There were even those Democrats who stood up and away from their party to support the liberty and freedom they knew I would fight to retain. Fighting together. Unwavering principled leadership was important to them, still is. I know this in my very being. God bless these brave men and women.

Why did those who worked against us fear me, fear my team? I could not be bought. I would not settle to operate according to the status quo losses of traditional past paths of my party, of all non-demmo parties in the state. I am a Republican, so were many of my volunteers and supporters. We are naturally innovative, not conventional, and knew we had to do things differently especially with resistance of some in my party. Off we went.

Pretty quickly out the gate we posted the need to fill vacant volunteer positions and the swamp came out in force! The naysayers, the insults, critiques, the negative swampy Nancy's all came out at once. They said there was no way we would fill our positions with volunteers, it couldn't be done – those were paid positions. Um, no. Boy were they wrong. In no time, the unlikely of folks started popping up. These were folks who had a fire in their bellies and fervor for restoration of California and our Republic. We call them the "Swamp Busters."

INDEX

[1] https://en.wikipedia.org/wiki/Moscone%E2%80%93Milk_assassinations

[2] https://play.google.com/store/apps/details?id=com.botsentinel&hl=en_US

[3] https://www.dailykos.com/stories/2018/5/22/1766317/-An-online-tool-to-check-Twitter-accounts-for-bots-trolls-and-fake-news

[4] "It" Reviews: https://www.screengeek.net/2017/06/22/graphic-sexual-content-involving-preteens-cut-it-movie/

[5] https://www.sacbee.com/news/politics-government/capitol-alert/article133464794.html

[6] https://www.kevindeleon.com/medicare-for-all-now/

[7] https://www.sacbee.com/news/politics-government/capitol-alert/article151960182.html

[8] https://feinsteinforca.com/issues/health-care

[9] https://www.congress.gov/bill/115th-congress/senate-bill/3036/text?format=txt&q=%7B%22search%22%3A%5B%22Ukraine+Act%22%5D%7D

[10] https://www.feinstein.senate.gov/public/index.cfm/immigration

[11] https://www.cbsnews.com/news/patrick-little-neo-nazi-senate-candidate-california-republican-convention/

[12] https://www.cbsnews.com/news/patrick-little-neo-nazi-senate-candidate-california-republican-convention/

[13] Did they split the steep cost of the table, reporting costs to the FEC? This candidate has not reported income to the FEC despite high filing costs, attending convention, having a table, and other costly events attended.

[14] https://www.sacbee.com/news/politics-government/capitol-alert/article210022244.html

[15] OANN, Interview with Patrick Hussein

[16] https://www.youtube.com/watch?v=ZDdurD46Al4

[17] https://gop.com/platform/

[18] https://democrats.org/about/party-platform/

[19] A group of weasels may be referred to as a "boogle," "confusion," "gang," or a "pack." http://www.havahart.com/weasel-facts

[20] November 1, 2018: https://en.wikipedia.org/wiki/Religion_and_politics_in_the_United_States

[21] Angel of Light: Name for the dynamo lady in our region who is so gracious and a great inspiration to those here in our quaint valley.

[22] https://en.oxforddictionaries.com/definition/tricky

[23] Wikipedia:
https://en.wikipedia.org/wiki/California_Proposition_14_(2010)
[24] October 3, 2018:
https://www.law.cornell.edu/constitution/first_amendment

ABOUT THE AUTHOR

Erin Cruz has dedicated the last decade to bring a conversation to the American Citizenry. Erin is known for her commentary, strategy, and analysis in multiple areas, with focus on conservative politics. Her commentary has been seen on Head Line News, MSNBC/NBC, Fox News, OANN, and on many nationally syndicated radio networks, and most importantly featured on New Media outlets, vlogs, and podcasts like New Right Network.

Erin's professional background covers, from the ground up, all areas of small and large business operations and administration in the private sector, as well as a solid stretch in academia covering safety and facilities management, business administration, accounting, payroll, personnel management, specialized and international human resources, domestic and international relations, with her favorite area of focus being domestic and international policy analysis and interpretation.

Most recently, Erin Cruz ran for public office in the State of California for the United States Senate, finishing 5th in a pool of 31 candidates in a state riddled with voter fraud and corruption. Traveling the state and campaigning, speaking to rooms with a hand full of people to thousands, Erin Cruz has been promoting communication, unity, and conservatism, journaling her experience.

Since the primary election Erin Cruz has been helping to promote candidates for elected office in California and across the nation on The Erin Cruz Show, where Erin is not only the Host she is also the Producer working with a small team of volunteers. She is looking to run for United States Senate in 2022 in the State of California. Her political leanings are freedom based. She is a constitutional conservative working to unite Americans Nation wide.   To find out more information, got to erincruz.com

www.ingramcontent.com/pod-product-compliance
Lightning Source LLC
Chambersburg PA
CBHW030447220526
45464CB00006B/2440